PREPOSTEROUS PETS

Compiled by Laura Cecil

Illustrated by Emma Chichester Clark

HAMISH HAMILTON
LONDON

ACKNOWLEDGEMENTS

Thanks are due to the following for permission to reprint copyright material: Peters Fraser & Dunlop Group Ltd for *The Yak* from COMPLETE VERSE by Hilaire Belloc, published by Pimlico, a division of Random Century. Copyright © Hilaire Belloc. Donald Bisset and Reed International Books for *Mr Smith's Hat* from TIGER WANTS MORE by Donald Bisset, published by Methuen Children's Books. Copyright © Donald Bisset. Laura Cecil for *The Flea*, retold by Laura Cecil from a Spanish folk tale. Copyright © Laura Cecil 1994. Faber and Faber Ltd for *The Story of Horace* by Alice M. Coats. Copyright © Alice M. Coats. Harcourt Brace & Company and Faber and Faber Ltd for *The Old Gumbie Cat* from OLD POSSUM'S BOOK OF PRACTICAL CATS by T. S. Eliot. Copyright © T. S. Eliot 1939, renewed 1967 by Esme Valerie Eliot. Macmillan Publishing Company and Faber and Faber Ltd for *My Brother Bert* from MEET MY FOLKS by Ted Hughes. Copyright © Ted Hughes 1961, 1973. Viking Kestrel Ltd and Murray Pollinger Ltd for *Out of the Oven* by Jan Mark. Copyright © Jan Mark 1985. A P Watt Ltd and Janet Alexander for *Miss Hegarty and the Beastie* by Janet McNeill. Copyright © Janet Alexander. André Deutsch Ltd and Little, Brown and Company for *The Tale of Custard the Dragon* from I WOULDN'T HAVE MISSED IT and VERSES FROM 1929 ON by Ogden Nash. Copyright © Ogden Nash 1936. David Higham Associates Ltd for *It Makes a Change* from RHYMES WITHOUT REASON by Mervyn Peake, published by Methuen Ltd. Copyright © Mervyn Peake 1944, this edition 1974. Philippa Pearce for *Emily's Own Elephant*, published by Walker Books Ltd & Greenwillow Books (a division of William Morrow, Inc., New York). Copyright © Philippa Pearce 1987. Greenwillow Books (a division of William Morrow, Inc., New York) for *The Multilingual Mynah Bird* from ZOO DOINGS by Jack Prelutsky. Copyright © Jack Prelutsky 1967, 1983. The James Reeves Estate for *If Pigs Could Fly* from THE COMPLETE POEMS FOR CHILDREN, published by Heinemann. Copyright © James Reeves 1959.

For Lucy
L.C.

HAMISH HAMILTON LTD

Published by the Penguin Group
27 Wrights Lane, London w8 5tz, England
Penguin Books USA Inc, 375 Hudson Street, New York, New York 10014, USA
Penguin Books Australia Ltd, Ringwood, Victoria, Australia
Penguin Books Canada Ltd, 10 Alcorn Avenue, Toronto, Ontario, Canada, m4v 3b2
Penguin Books (NZ) Ltd, 182–190 Wairau Road, Auckland 10, New Zealand

Penguin Books Ltd, Registered Offices: Harmondsworth, Middlesex, England

First published in Great Britain 1994 by Hamish Hamilton Ltd

This collection copyright © 1994 by Laura Cecil
Illustrations copyright © 1994 by Emma Chichester Clark

1 3 5 7 9 10 8 6 4 2

The moral rights of the author and artist have been asserted.

British Library Cataloguing in Publication Data
CIP data for this book is available from the British Library

ISBN 0-241-00253-2

Photoset by Rowland Phototypesetting Ltd
Bury St Edmunds, Suffolk
Printed in Hong Kong by
Imago Services

CONTENTS

My Brother Bert

TED HUGHES

Pets are the Hobby of my Brother Bert.
He used to go to school with a Mouse in his shirt.

His Hobby it grew, as some hobbies will,
And grew and GREW and GREW until –

Oh don't breathe a word, pretend you haven't heard.
A simply appalling thing has occurred –

The very thought makes me iller and iller:
Bert's brought home a gigantic Gorilla!

If you think that's really not such a scare,
What if it quarrels with his Grizzly Bear?

You still think you could keep your head?
What if the Lion from under the bed

And the four Ostriches that deposit
Their football eggs in his bedroom closet

And the Aardvark out of his bottom drawer
All danced out and joined in the Roar?

What if the Pangolins were to caper
Out of their nests behind the wallpaper?

With the fifty sorts of Bats
That hang on his hatstand like old hats,

And out of a shoebox the excitable Platypus
Along with the Ocelot or Jungle-Cattypus?

The Wombat, the Dingo, the Gecko, the Grampus –
How they would shake the house with their Rumpus!

Not to forget the Bandicoot
Who would certainly peer from his battered old boot.

Why it could be a dreadful day,
And what Oh what would the neighbours say!

Mr Smith's Hat

DONALD BISSET

Once upon a time there was a man named John Smith who bought a new hat. He put it on and went for a walk in the park. It was a very windy day and the wind blew his hat off.

It went right up in the air, over the trees and houses and over the hills and far away, and was never heard of again.

So Mr Smith went and bought another hat. And the wind blew *it* away too, right up over the hills and far away, and it was never heard of again.

So Mr Smith went and bought *another* hat. But this time he didn't put it on. He went home and got a glue pot and put some glue all round the hat inside, and round his head. Then he put the hat on and waited for the glue to dry.

"The wind will never blow it off now!" said Mr Smith.

Just then Mrs Smith came in with the tea and they sat down to eat. "Aren't you going to take your hat off?" asked Mrs Smith.

"No," said Mr Smith, "it's glued on."

That evening at bath time, Mr Smith wore his hat in the bath and it got all wet.

And then he went to bed in his hat. Mrs Smith *was* surprised.

In the morning, when he was leaving for the office, Mrs Smith said, "Have you combed your hair, John?"

"No," said Mr Smith. "I can't with my hat on."

"You mustn't go to the office without combing your hair," said Mrs Smith.

Well, since Mr Smith *couldn't* comb his hair, he didn't go to the office. He went back to bed. And he stayed there for twenty years and read the papers. It *was* nice! – especially on Mondays.

But at last he got tired of staying in bed, and said to

his wife, "My dear, when you go to the shops today please buy me a hippopotamus and a long piece of thick rope like sailors use for tying ships to the quayside. Oh, and you'd better buy me a ton of hay and some apples and carrots in case the hippopotamus is hungry."

So Mrs Smith went to the pet shop.

"Good morning, Mrs Smith," said the man. "What can I do for you this morning? Would you like to buy a budgerigar?"

"No thank you," said Mrs Smith, "I want a – "

"Dog?" said the man.

"No!" said Mrs Smith.

"A monkey?"

"No thank you."

"A mouse or a hamster?"

"No!"

"A koala bear?"

"No!"

"A parrot, then? Or a mynah bird?"

"Oh no!" said Mrs Smith. "I want a – "

"A tortoise?" said the man.

"No, no, no! I want a – "

"Pussycat?"

"Please – don't interrupt!" said Mrs Smith. "I want a hippopotamus."

"Oh dear," said the man, "I'm not sure that we've got one. I'll go and look."

He came back a few minutes later. "We *have* got one, Mrs Smith," he said. "Here he is. His name is Henry. That'll be £156 please."

"Thank you," said Mrs Smith, "and I want a ton of hay and a big bag of apples and carrots and please have them sent round to our house. I'll take Henry with me. I expect he'd like a walk. And I want a big piece of rope as well."

When Mrs Smith got home Mr Smith was very pleased and got out of bed and went out and climbed on

Henry's back and had Mrs Smith tie his legs together under Henry's tummy. Then he set off for a ride in the park.

"Good morning, Mr Smith," said the people he passed. "How nice to see you again. We haven't seen you for a long time."

They passed the grocer's and the fishmonger's and the post office till they came to the church just outside the park.

"Good morning, Mr Smith," said the vicar when he saw him. "Delightful weather we're having." But just then the wind swooped down and blew the vicar's hat off over the houses, over the trees and over the hills and far away.

The wind tried to blow Mr Smith's hat away. But it couldn't because it was glued on so tight. Then the wind blew harder and harder and harder and tried to blow Mr Smith away. But it couldn't because he was tied tight to Henry.

It blew and it blew and it *blew*. But it couldn't blow Mr Smith away and it couldn't blow Henry away. He was much too big.

Mr Smith was very pleased and after that he stopped staying in bed every day and went for a ride on Henry instead. And the wind never blew his hat away again.

The Tale of Custard the Dragon

Ogden Nash

Belinda lived in a little white house,
With a little black kitten and a little grey mouse,
And a little yellow dog and a little red wagon,
And a realio, trulio, little pet dragon.

Now the name of the little black kitten was Ink,
And the little grey mouse, she called him Blink,
And the little yellow dog was sharp as Mustard,
But the dragon was a coward, and she
    called him Custard.

Custard the dragon had big sharp teeth,
And spikes on top of him and scales underneath,
Mouth like a fireplace, chimney for a nose,
And realio, trulio daggers on his toes.

Belinda was as brave as a barrel full of bears,
And Ink and Blink chased lions down the stairs,
Mustard was as brave as a tiger in a rage,
But Custard cried for a nice safe cage.

Belinda tickled him, she tickled him unmerciful,
Ink, Blink and Mustard, they rudely
    called him Percival,

They all sat laughing in the little red wagon
At the realio, trulio, cowardly dragon.

Belinda giggled till she shook the house,
And Blink said Weeck! which is giggling
  for a mouse,
Ink and Mustard rudely asked his age,
When Custard cried for a nice safe cage.

Suddenly, suddenly they heard a nasty sound,
And Mustard growled, and they all looked around.
Meowch! cried Ink, and Ooh! cried Belinda,
For there was a pirate, climbing in the winda.

Pistol in his left hand, pistol in his right,
And he held in his teeth a cutlass bright,
His beard was black, one leg was wood;
It was clear that the pirate meant no good.

Belinda paled, and she cried Help! Help!
But Mustard fled with a terrified yelp,
Ink trickled down to the bottom of the household,
And little mouse Blink strategically mouseholed.

But up jumped Custard, snorting like an engine,
Clashed his tail like irons in a dungeon,
With a clatter and a clank and a jangling squirm,
He went at the pirate like a robin at a worm.

The pirate gaped at Belinda's dragon,
And gulped some grog from his pocket flagon,
He fired two bullets, but they didn't hit,
And Custard gobbled him, every bit.

Belinda embraced him, Mustard licked him,
No one mourned for his pirate victim.
Ink and Blink in glee did gyrate
Around the dragon that ate the pirate.

But presently up spoke little dog Mustard,
I'd have been twice as brave if I hadn't been flustered.
And up spoke Ink and up spoke Blink,
We'd have been three times as brave, we think,
And Custard said, I quite agree
That everybody is braver than me.

Belinda still lives in her little white house,
With her little black kitten and her little grey mouse.
And her little yellow dog and her little red wagon,
And her realio, trulio little pet dragon.

Belinda is as brave as a barrel full of bears,
And Ink and Blink chase lions down the stairs,
Mustard is as brave as a tiger in a rage,
But Custard keeps crying for a nice safe cage.

The Story of Horace

ALICE M. COATS

Once upon a time there was a family who lived together in a little house in a wood. There was Great-grandpa, Great-grandma, Grandpa, Grandma, Pa, Ma, Paul and little Lulu. And with them lived Horace. Horace was a bear!

One day Pa went out hunting. And on the way back he was met by Great-grandma, Grandpa, Grandma, Ma, Paul and little Lulu. And they all said, "What do you think has happened?"

And Pa said, "What has happened?"

And they said, "Horace has eaten Great-grandpa!"

And Pa was just wild, and he said, "I will kill Horace!" But they all took on so he hadn't the heart to do it.

And the next day Pa went out hunting. And on the way back he was met by Grandpa, Grandma, Ma, Paul and little Lulu. And they all said, "What do you think has happened?"

And Pa said, "What has happened?"

And they said, "Horace has eaten Great-grandma!"

And Pa was just wild, and he said, "I will kill Horace!" But they all took on so he hadn't the heart to do it.

And the next day Pa went out hunting. And on the way back he was met by Grandma, Ma, Paul and little Lulu. And they all said, "What do you think has happened?"

And Pa said, "What has happened?"

And they said, "Horace has eaten Grandpa!"

And Pa was just wild, and he said, "I will kill Horace!" But they all took on so he hadn't the heart to do it.

And the next day Pa went out hunting. And on the way back he was met by Ma, Paul and little Lulu. And they all said, "What do you think has happened?"

And Pa said, "What has happened?"

And they said, "Horace has eaten Grandma!"

And Pa was just wild, and he said, "I will kill Horace!" But they all took on so he hadn't the heart to do it.

And the next day Pa went out hunting. And on the way back he was met by Paul and little Lulu. And they both said, "What do you think has happened?"

And Pa said, "What has happened?"

And they said, "Horace has eaten Ma!"

And Pa was just wild, and he said, "I will kill Horace!" But they both took on so he hadn't the heart to do it.

And the next day Pa went out hunting. And on the way back he was met by little Lulu. And little Lulu said, "What do you think has happened?"

And Pa said, "What has happened?"

And little Lulu said, "Horace has eaten Paul!"

And Pa was just wild, and he said, "I will kill Horace!" But little Lulu took on so he hadn't the heart to do it.

And the next day Pa went out hunting. And on the way back he was met by Horace. And Horace said, "What do you think has happened?"

And Pa said, "What has happened?"

And Horace said, "I've eaten little Lulu!"

And Pa was just wild, and he said, "I will kill you, Horace!" But Horace took on so he hadn't the heart to do it.

And the next day HORACE went out hunting!

It Makes a Change

MERVYN PEAKE

There's nothing makes a Greenland Whale
Feel half so high-and-mighty,
As sitting on a mantelpiece
In Aunty Mabel's nighty.

It makes a change from Freezing Seas,
(Of which a Whale can tire),
To warm his weary tail at ease
Before an English fire.

For this delight he leaves the sea,
(Unknown to Aunty Mabel),
Returning only when the dawn
Lights up the Breakfast Table.

The Flea

A Spanish Folktale
Retold by Laura Cecil

There was once a King of Spain called King Felipe. He loved making jokes and asking riddles.

One morning, when he was putting on his robes, a flea jumped out of his collar and landed on his cheek. Immediately he clapped his hand over it, and laughed aloud:

"Whoever heard of a King having a flea? What a delightfully absurd idea! We must treat this flea with honour, for now she has bitten the King, she has royal blood!"

Then he turned to his courtiers and asked them what should be done with the flea. Nobody knew what to say, until the court Jester spoke:

"Your Majesty, why don't you put her in a cage and fatten her up? When she has grown large enough, make her skin into a tambourine as a present for your daughter, Princess Belita."

"Excellent," laughed the King. "But I have an even better idea. The Princess shall dance to the tambourine, and any man who can guess what skin it is made from, shall marry her. We shall invent a beautiful riddle to ask the suitors."

The King called the royal flea Felipa. She was put in a golden cage as large as a field. After a week she was as fat as a rat; in a month she was as fat as a cat; in two months she was as big as a pig and at the end of four months she was as big as Princess Belita. So King Felipe ordered that Felipa should be killed and made into a large tambourine. First her skin was stretched and put out in the sun to dry. Then it was pummelled, until it was soft enough to be made into the finest tambourine in Spain. It had golden bells and many-coloured ribbons hanging from it.

Every time a suitor came to woo the Princess she would dance, tapping out the rhythm on the tambourine and shaking the golden bells. Then the King would recite the riddle:

"Felipa and Belita – see how they dance together!
Felipa and Belita – now can you tell me whether
You can say what it is, this creature called Felipa?
If you answer me right, you marry Belita."

Princes and dukes came from everywhere, but although they guessed the riddle was about the tambourine, they always thought it was made of goat or sheep skin. Then the King would roar with laughter and shout, "You are wrong!"

But after a while King Felipe got bored and he announced that any suitor, who could not guess the riddle, would be hanged. After that all the dukes and princes stayed away.

But there was a young shepherd boy, called Manuel, who lived in the hills outside the city. He heard about the riddle and decided to try his luck. He was not clever, but he liked the idea of marrying a princess and living in a palace.

"You are crazy!" said his mother. "Nobody can guess the King's riddle. You'll just be hanged!"   ·

But the boy was stubborn and said he would go. So his mother gave up nagging and made him a tortilla to eat on the journey.

As Manuel was walking along he heard a tiny voice shouting at him from under his boot.

"Please don't tread on me!"

He looked down and saw a tiny black ant.

"Give me a ride to the city in your bag, shepherd boy," pleaded the ant.

"As long as you don't nibble my tortilla," answered Manuel, and he picked up the ant and put her in his bag, after the ant had agreed to dust her six little feet.

A little later, Manuel felt a tickling on his leg. He looked down and saw a green beetle trying to climb up.

"Shepherd boy, give me a ride to the city in your bag."

"Certainly, as long as you don't nibble my tortilla."

So the beetle joined the ant in Manuel's bag.

A little later Manuel heard a noise by his ear. He looked down and saw a little grey mouse on his shoulder.

"Shepherd boy, give me a ride in your bag," she squeaked.

"No, you will break my tortilla that I want to have for lunch," said Manuel.

"Why don't we eat it all together now? Then afterwards I can ride in your bag to the city," answered the mouse.

So Manuel sat down with the ant, the beetle and the mouse and they ate the tortilla. Then Manuel remembered why he was making his journey and suddenly he felt very frightened.

"Why are you shivering?" asked the ant, the beetle and the mouse.

"I am going to see the King. He will ask me a riddle and if I get it right I shall marry Princess Belita, but if I get it wrong I shall be hanged," answered Manuel.

"Don't worry," said the ant, the beetle and the mouse. "We owe you a good turn. One of us is sure to know the answer."

So Manuel set off slowly to the city with his three friends riding in his bag. "Get a move on, Manuel!" they called. "It is getting hot in here!"

At last Manuel reached the palace. A splendid guard, dressed in a scarlet uniform, stood outside the gate.

"Please will you take me to the King," said Manuel nervously. "I have come to answer the riddle."

The guard sighed and shrugged his shoulders as he led Manuel to the Throne room.

"That shepherd boy must be a fool," he thought. "He is certain to be hanged."

When King Felipe saw Manuel's poor clothes, his patched cloak and his battered leather bag, he said,

"Shepherd boy, it is better to be alive, even if you are poor. An ignorant boy like you won't know the answer to my riddle. Go home to your sheep."

But Manuel was stubborn. "A shepherd boy has as much right as a prince to answer your riddle. I shall stay here until you let me try!"

"Very well," said the King. "Don't say I didn't warn you."

So Princess Belita danced with her tambourine while the King recited:

"Felipa and Belita – see how they dance together!
Felipa and Belita – now can you tell me whether
You can say what it is, this creature called Felipa?
If you answer me right, you marry Belita,
If you answer me wrong, you won't live long."

When the song was over, Manuel took the tambourine and peered at it closely.

"Please help me, little friends," he whispered. "I know what sheep or goat skin is like. It isn't either of those."

"Let me have a look," said the ant.

Nobody saw her crawl out of Manuel's bag and on to his hand. He placed her on the tambourine and she quickly ran over its surface. Almost immediately she was back on his hand.

"Whatever its size – it is a flea. I would know one anywhere!" she whispered to him.

"Stop dithering, shepherd boy!" cried the King. "What is your answer?"

"It's a flea, your Majesty," said Manuel.

There was silence and then a gasp of shock and amazement from all the courtiers. "The princess *can't* marry a shepherd boy," they murmured.

Princess Belita stamped her foot. "I *won't* marry this grubby little shepherd boy!" she said and burst into loud sobs.

"My dearest Belita, of course you won't," said the King.

"I can't say I like her much either, but I'm the one to say whether she will or won't marry me," said Manuel. "You promised the hand of your daughter to anyone who answered the riddle."

"I will promise you *anything* else you want," pleaded Princess Belita.

"So will I," said King Felipe.

"Very well. I would like a cart, so that I can ride home in comfort," began Manuel.

"With two white oxen to pull it," whispered the beetle.

"With two white oxen to pull it," added Manuel.

"It shall be as you wish," said the King.

"And what shall I give you?" said Princess Belita.

"Ask her to fill your bag to the brim with gold," whispered the mouse.

Well, that didn't sound very much, so the Princess happily ordered the gold to be brought to the Throne room. But when they started to pour the gold into the bag, it never filled, because the gold ran straight through the bottom on to the floor. The Mouse had gnawed a big hole when no one was looking! Soon Manuel was standing up to his knees in gold.

"That'll do," said he after a while, when there was enough to fill his cart.

When the ox-cart was piled high with gold, Manuel and his three friends drove back to his home in the hills. He was now so rich, he did not need to work again. He bought a fine house and married a shepherd's pretty daughter. They spent their nights dancing, and their days dozing on their veranda and eating Turkish Delight.

A happy life – if that is what you like.

The Old Gumbie Cat

T. S. Eliot

I have a Gumbie Cat in mind, her name is
 Jennyanydots;
Her coat is of the tabby kind, with tiger stripes and
 leopard spots.
All day she sits upon the stair or on the steps or on
 the mat:
She sits and sits and sits and sits – and that's what
 makes a Gumbie Cat!

But when the day's hustle and bustle is done,
Then the Gumbie Cat's work is but hardly begun.
And when all the family's in bed and asleep,
She tucks up her skirts to the basement to creep.
She is deeply concerned with the ways
of the mice –
Their behaviour's not good and their manners
not nice;
So when she has got them lined up on the matting,
She teaches them music, crocheting and tatting.

I have a Gumbie Cat in mind, her name is
    Jennyanydots;
Her equal would be hard to find, she likes the warm
    and sunny spots.
All day she sits beside the hearth or in the sun or on
    my hat:
She sits and sits and sits and sits – and that's what
    makes a Gumbie Cat!

But when the day's hustle and bustle is done,
Then the Gumbie Cat's work is but hardly begun.
As she finds that the mice will not ever keep quiet,
She is sure it is due to irregular diet
And believing that nothing is done without trying,
She sets right to work with her baking and frying.
She makes them a mouse-cake of bread and
    dried peas,
And a *beautiful* fry of lean bacon and cheese.

I have a Gumbie Cat in mind, her name is
    Jennyanydots;
The curtain-cord she likes to wind, and tie it into
    sailor-knots.
She sits upon the window-sill, or anything that's
    smooth and flat:

She sits and sits and sits and sits – and that's what
  makes a Gumbie Cat!

  But when the day's hustle and bustle is done,
  Then the Gumbie Cat's work is but hardly begun.
  She thinks that the cockroaches
      just need employment
  To prevent them from idle and
      wanton destroyment.
  So she's formed, from that lot of disorderly louts,
  A troop of well-disciplined helpful boy-scouts,
  With a purpose in life and a good deed to do –
  And she's even created a Beetles' Tattoo.

So for Old Gumbie Cats let us now give
    three cheers –
On whom well-ordered households depend,
  it appears.

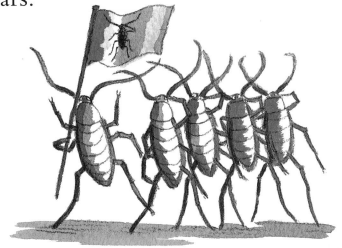

Emily's Own Elephant

PHILIPPA PEARCE

Emily lived with her mother and father in a little house in the corner of a big meadow. A river ran along one side of the meadow.

Huge trees grew in the meadow. There were oaks and chestnuts and sycamores and ash-trees. Emily's father used to say: "There are far too many trees in the meadow. Perhaps I should cut some of them down."

His wife said: "You haven't enough to do in your spare time. That's why you want to go cutting trees down."

A big shed stood in the meadow. It was old, but it was not in ruins. There were no holes in the roof for the rain to come through. There were no holes in the walls for the wind to blow through. The shed was quite empty. It was not used for anything.

Emily's father said: "Perhaps I should pull that useless shed down."

Emily's mother said: "You haven't enough to do in your spare time. That's why you want to go pulling sheds down."

Emily said: "Don't cut the trees down. Don't pull the

shed down. You never know when we may need trees and an empty shed."

Emily's father promised not to cut down the trees or pull down the shed just yet.

One day in winter Emily went to London to visit the Zoo. She went with her mother. They saw all the animals that Emily liked best: the lions, the tigers, the hippos, the rhinos, the camels, the giraffes, the elephants, the wolves and the panda-bear.

Then it was time for tea, and they went to the cafeteria. Emily's mother had a pot of tea and a packet of biscuits, and Emily had an ice-cream and a packet of potato crisps.

When they had finished tea, Emily's mother said: "It's nearly time to go home. Is there anything else you very much want to see, Emily?"

"Yes," said Emily. "I want to go to the Children's Zoo."

So they went to the Children's Zoo. They saw the rabbits and Emily stroked one. They watched the chickens hatching out of eggs.

They visited the goats, and Emily fed one with a sandwich. The goat ate a paper-bag, and then it tried to eat the glove on the hand that had held the sandwich and the paper-bag.

Then Emily and her mother came to a special enclosure with a baby elephant in it. It was the nicest elephant that Emily had ever seen.

A keeper was standing by the elephant's enclosure. Emily asked him: "What is the baby elephant called?"

"Jumbo," said the keeper.

"Jumbo!" said Emily's mother. "What a nice name. Now Emily, it's time to go home."

The keeper said to Emily: "We are very worried

about Jumbo."

"Why?" said Emily.

"Come along, Emily," said her mother.

The keeper said to Emily: "We are worried about Jumbo because he doesn't grow. He is strong and he is healthy, but he simply won't grow. He is going to be a miniature elephant."

"I didn't know that elephants could be miniature," said Emily.

"*Come along, Emily*," said her mother.

"It happens only very, very rarely," said the keeper. "But it is always very awkward. The Zoo wants only elephants that are elephantine in size. It can't keep a miniature elephant."

"Oh," said Emily.

"COME ALONG, EMILY," said her mother.

"We shall have to find a home for Jumbo," said the keeper.

"*EMILY!*" said Emily's mother very loudly and crossly.

Emily usually did what her mother told her, especially as her mother usually told her to do only sensible things. So now Emily began to follow her mother out of the Children's Zoo.

Then Emily stopped. "I'm sorry," she said to her mother, "but we can't go home yet. I have an important idea. I must discuss it with the keeper. I must go back now." So back they went.

They went back to the baby elephant's enclosure. The keeper was still standing there. He was looking at Jumbo in a worried way. Emily said: "You told us that you would have to find a home for Jumbo."

"Yes," said the keeper.

"We could give him a home," said Emily, and she looked at her mother.

Emily's mother said to the keeper: "My daughter is quite right. We should be delighted to give your little elephant a home."

The keeper said: "That's very kind of you; but even a miniature elephant needs a great deal of space."

"Would a big meadow do?" asked Emily's mother.

"A really big meadow," said Emily.

"Yes," said the keeper, "a really big meadow would do. But even a miniature elephant needs a lot of water to drink and to bathe in and to squirt around when it plays."

"Would a river running by the meadow do?" Emily asked.

"Yes," said the keeper, "a river would do. But what about when it rains – what about when it rains bucketfuls and blows gales? The little elephant will need shelter then."

"Would a shed in the meadow do?" asked Emily.

"A really big shed," said her mother. "It has no holes in the roof or the walls, and it's quite empty."

"Yes," said the keeper, "a really big shed would do."

"Then that's settled," said Emily's mother.

"Wait!" said the keeper. "What about when it snows and freezes: would your shed be warm enough for a little elephant then?"

"No," said Emily. "Our shed hasn't a coal-fire; it hasn't a gas-fire; it hasn't an electric fire."

"Wait," said Emily's mother. "We could put in central heating."

"Wouldn't that be very expensive?" said Emily.

"It would be worth it," said her mother. "It's not often anyone has the chance of a baby elephant that will stay small."

"That's settled then," said the keeper. "We are very grateful to you. There's just one more thing."

"What is that?"

"Jumbo will be lonely without any of his friends," said the keeper. "Could you take one of his friends as well?"

"What kind of friend?" asked Emily's mother.

"His best friend is a baby monkey called Jacko. He likes climbing," said the keeper.

"Then he can climb all the trees in the meadow," said Emily's mother.

"I've always longed for a little elephant and a monkey," said Emily.

"When they are old enough," said the keeper, "Jumbo and Jacko will come to you in a special Zoo van. Please write your name and address on this paper."

So they did, and then they went home.

One Saturday in summer Emily's father was eating toast and marmalade and looking out of the window.

Suddenly he spoke with his mouth full: "There is a big van, like a horse-box, at the gate into our meadow. Two men are driving the van into our meadow. Now they are opening the van. Something is coming out. OH! OH! OH!" Emily's father nearly choked on his toast and marmalade. He said: "There is an elephant in our meadow, with a monkey on its back."

Then Emily and her mother told him all about Jumbo and Jacko. They had been keeping the secret to surprise him. He was delighted. He said: "We must be sure to have the central heating in the shed before next winter. I will put it in myself. That will save expense."

"It will also give you something to do in your spare time," said his wife.

Then they all went into the meadow with buns for the elephant and bananas for the monkey. They took a pot of tea for the Zoo men, and a big plum cake that happened to be in the house. There was a slice for everybody, and sugar biscuits too, and chocolate fingers. They all had a picnic together in the sunshiny meadow.

Then the Zoo men said goodbye and went home. Emily's mother went indoors to make more buns.

Emily's father went up the village to the Public Library to borrow a book about central heating.

Emily was left alone in the meadow with Jumbo and Jacko. It was very hot, so Emily led the way to the river. Jumbo waded in the cool water and squirted it over his friends. They loved this.

Then Jacko went racing through the tree-tops. He picked armfuls of pink and white blossom from the very tops of the chestnut-trees. It was the biggest and best chestnut blossom that Emily had ever seen. She made wreaths and garlands and chains of it for Jumbo and Jacko and herself.

Then they began to dance round and round the meadow. Emily's mother finished baking her buns and came into the meadow to watch. Emily's father came home with his book on central heating and went into the meadow, too. Emily's father and mother stood and watched and laughed and clapped. And round and round the meadow danced Emily and her two friends from the Zoo.

The Multilingual Mynah Bird

Jack Prelutsky

Birds are known to cheep and chirp
and sing and warble, peep and purp,
and some can only squeak and squawk,
but the mynah bird is able to talk.

The mynah bird, the mynah bird,
a major, not a minor bird;
you'll never find a finer bird
than the multilingual mynah bird.

He can talk to you in Japanese,
Italian, French and Portuguese:
and even Russian and Chinese
the mynah bird will learn with ease.

The multilingual mynah bird
can say most any word he's heard,
and sometimes he invents a few
(a very difficult thing to do).

So if you want to buy a bird,
why don't you try the mynah bird?
You'll never find a finer bird
than the multilingual mynah bird.

Out of the Oven

JAN MARK

Matty went to live with her grandmother. Gran was making bread. She put it in the oven and closed the door.

"Don't you open that door until I tell you," said Gran, "or the devils will get out."

"Where are the devils?" Matty asked.

"In the oven," said Gran. "Where else? Devils like to be hot."

"I thought devils were big and hairy," said Matty.

Gran said, "These are baby devils. They are small and furry."

"Like kittens?"

"Yes," said Gran, "but they have little horns. You leave them be or the bread won't rise."

Matty watched the oven each time Gran opened the door, but no little devils came out. Queenie, the cat, caught mice every night and laid them on the rag mat, so that Gran would know she was earning her keep. She never caught any little devils. Queenie had kittens.

Gran said they were like little devils, but they had no horns.

One day Gran took the bread out of the oven and forgot to shut the door.

That night Matty woke up in the dark and heard little footsteps. She went downstairs in her nightgown and looked round the kitchen door, and there were the little devils, playing on the rag mat. Their eyes were like the sparks that flew when Gran sharpened her carving knife on the chimney breast.

When they saw Matty the little devils sprang back into the oven and pulled the door to – all but one. Left behind was the littlest devil of all, and when he saw that the others had gone without him he put out his claws, as fine as white eyelashes, and cried like a kitten, *meeow, meeow*. Queenie left her mousehole, picked up the little

devil by the scruff of his neck, and carried him to her basket where he curled up among the kittens and went to sleep.

Next morning Matty looked into the basket to see if there really was a little devil in it. There was.

"Put him back in the oven at once," said Gran.

"Can't we keep him?" Matty asked. Gran shook her head, and put out her hand to grab the little devil, but Queenie stood up and arched her back, and slitted her eyes, and swelled, and swore. Her tail went round and round like a sycamore seed.

Gran knew when to leave well alone. "You can keep him for now," she said, "but if I get my hands on him, back in the oven he goes!"

Queenie taught the little devil to be a good little kitten.

The little devil taught the kittens to be devilish little kittens. They learned very quickly. They learned to ski down the curtains . . . and to skate on the butter. At Christmas they got into the turkey . . .

Because he no longer lived in the hot oven, the little devil grew very furry, all over, and no one would have known that he was a little devil, but for the tiny horns on his head.

Gran still wanted to put him back in the oven, but Matty said it would be cruel. "He's too furry now to live in

the oven," said Matty.

"Furry or not, he's still a little devil," said Gran, but she did not put him back in the oven. She could not catch him. By now he could run and jump and go straight up trees, just like a real cat. Matty called him Tiddles, and hoped that Gran would forget he was a little devil.

Soon Tiddles stopped being a *little* devil and grew quite large. When spring came he sat on the doorstep in the sun, with his paws tucked under and his tail curled round to the front, and purred. Beside him sat the kittens who were growing into big cats, and Queenie, who was already a big cat. Gran looked at them and clicked her teeth. "Enough is enough," said Gran. "That lot drink more milk than they're worth."

She found good homes for the kittens in the village, and then she went to fetch the little devil. "It's back in the oven with you, my lad," said Gran.

Tiddles blinked his green eyes and streaked to the top of the pear tree. "Just wait till he comes down," said Gran, "I can't keep a lumping great devil in my house. What would the vicar say?" Matty thought that she could deal with the vicar.

The fifth Sunday after Easter is Rogation-tide, when the animals go to church.

Gran put on her hat and went off to church with Queenie. Matty brushed the little devil, and fluffed up his fur to hide the horns, and put him in a basket. Then she went to church, too.

Tiddles sat on the grating where the warm air comes up and said, "Meeow meeow," when everyone else said, "Amen amen."

"That's a fine figure of a cat you have there," the vicar said, after the service.

"Thank you, sir," said Matty.

The vicar stroked the little devil between the ears and looked surprised.

"Are you sure it's a cat?" said the vicar.

"He's called Tiddles," said Matty.

"Well, he's certainly a . . . fine figure of a cat," said the vicar.

"You can't put him back in the oven now," Matty said to Gran, when they got home. "Not after he's been to church."

The little devil remembered the grating where the warm air comes up, and he went to church every Sunday, after that. No more was said about putting him back in the oven.

When summer came, Tiddles washed his whiskers and polished his horns and went courting; and in September his wife had three kittens. One was as tabby as tar and coal smoke, one was orange and white, like marigolds in snow, and one was black. Matty watched the black kitten and often stroked him between the ears. One day she found two little knobs there, like rivets, and she knew that his horns were coming.

"Now we have another little devil," said Matty. She called him Puss, so that no one should guess.

In time, Matty grew up, and Tiddles grew old, and one day he folded his paws and passed peacefully away. Matty made him a nice grave by the coal shed where it was sheltered and sunny, even in winter, and Puss took his father's place on the doorstep. By now there were quite a lot of little devils in the village. Their fame spread. Scholars and other learned persons came to look at them, and make notes.

"Are you sure these are cats?" said the scholars, stroking them between the ears.

"Of course they are cats," snapped Gran. "They catch mice, don't they?"

"They look more like little devils to me," said a learned lady.

"If that's what you think," said Matty, "come to church on Sunday and see what's what."

So the learned persons came to church and saw what

was what. All the little devils were there, lined up on the warm-air grating by the chancel arch.

"Whoever heard of devils going to church?" said a scholar to the learned lady, and left immediately to catch the stopping train to London, which was all that ran on Sundays.

"Whoever heard of *cats* going to church?" asked the learned lady, but her remark was lost in the scuffle as the rest of the scholars hurried off to the station.

The little devils sat in a row on the grating and purred devoutly, louder than the organ and sweeter than the choir. The sun shone clear through a stained-glass saint, and gilded their horns.

The Yak

HILAIRE BELLOC

As a friend to the children, commend me the yak;
  You will find it exactly the thing:
It will carry and fetch, you can ride on its back,
  Or lead it about with a string.

The Tartar who dwells in the plains of Tibet
　　(A desolate region of snow),
Has for centuries made it a nursery pet,
　　And surely the Tartar should know!

Then tell your papa where the yak can be got,
　　And if he is awfully rich,
He will buy you the creature – or else he will *not*:
　　I cannot be positive which.

63

Miss Hegarty and the Beastie

JANET MCNEILL

When anybody in the village wanted to buy anything at all they went to Miss Hegarty's shop because there was no other shop to go to. The little bell above the door said "ping!" as soon as the door was opened, and Miss Hegarty came out of her parlour at the back and said, "Good day to you and what is it you want?" And whatever it was, flour or shoelaces, candles or thread, butter or a mousetrap, Miss Hegarty knew where to look for it. "And what else do you want?" she asked, and if there was anything else she knew where to find that too. "Take your time now, don't hurry," Miss Hegarty always said to her customers, "I'm sure there is something else you want, and you'll think of it in a moment or two." And very often that is just what they did. "If you want it, Miss Hegarty's got it," they said up in the village.

One evening, just at six o'clock when Miss Hegarty was ready to shut up the shop, she heard the little bell saying "ping!" but she didn't look up straight away. She was busy counting out the florins and the shillings, the sixpences, the threepenny pieces and the pennies into tall neat piles. But when at last she did look up to see who it was, there was no one there. So she waited, thinking it was one of the children who was too small to see over the counter. She expected to see a little hand raised and a penny set down, and to hear a voice asking for a gobstopper or a stick of chewing gum. "Well now," she said, "and what is it you want?"

No hand appeared. No one answered her. So Miss Hegarty leaned across the counter and looked – and she saw the beastie. He was a low, round, fat, happy beastie, and he was lying close up against the counter. The yellow sunlight was shining on him and he had his eyes shut.

Miss Hegarty might have been afraid of a mouse but she wasn't afraid of a beastie.

"Well now," she said again, "and what *is* it you want?"

The beastie opened his eyes and looked at her. His eyes were green, like wet green lollipops when the sun shines through them.

"I don't want anything," the beastie said. "Thank you very much for asking, I'm sure," and he closed his eyes again.

"You don't want anything?" cried Miss Hegarty. "Oh, but you must want something!"

He kept his eyes shut and asked, "Why?"

"Everybody wants something. That's why they come here. If you open your eyes again and look round the shop you'll soon remember what it is you want."

He opened his eyes slowly and looked. He looked at the shelves that covered every wall, reaching from floor to ceiling. They were filled with bags of sugar and packets of tea and boxes of buttons and tins of sardines. He looked above his head at the ceiling, which was hung more thickly than any Christmas tree with sauce-pans, buckets, sausages, shovels and bedroom slippers. He stretched up to look at the counter, packed with postcards, pens, pencils, matches, ink and blotting-paper. He bent down and looked at the floor of the shop where sacks of flour leaned against bags of dog biscuits and bundles of firewood were propped beside a box of oranges.

"Now," said Miss Hegarty, "you've had a look. What is it you want?"

The beastie didn't answer, but stared and shrugged his shoulders which were black and shiny, like a plastic waterproof when it has been raining.

"A toothbrush, perhaps?"

The beastie opened his mouth very wide and showed her the large pink cave inside his large pink mouth.

There wasn't a tooth to be seen; he couldn't want a toothbrush.

"Shoelaces, then?"

But the beastie stretched out one of his six fat paws (with seven toes on each of them) and there were no shoes, and so no need for any shoelaces.

"Soap?" Miss Hegarty said, but this was a silly question for she could see for herself that he was as clean as if he'd just come straight out of the bath.

Miss Hegarty was puzzled – and cross. She began to guess other things that the beastie might want: "Scissors – a fourpenny stamp – a packet of cornflakes – I've got some packets with cowboy masks on them; you'd like that, wouldn't you?"

The beastie blew out his cheeks – pouf! – and said, "I've got a face of my own, thank you very much."

"Of course you have a face," said Miss Hegarty, "and a very handsome face it is, too. But there must be something you want. Just stay here very quietly and think of all the things you haven't got; you'll soon find out that you want one of them."

So the beastie sat very quietly in the sunlight, thinking. Miss Hegarty locked the money in a drawer and pulled down the blinds of the shop and swept the floor. Then she put the brush into the cupboard and came back. "Well," she asked, "and have you remembered?"

The beastie yawned very wide and said, "I don't want anything at all."

"This is ridiculous," Miss Hegarty snapped—she was getting hungry for her tea. "Everyone who comes here wants something."

"And when they've got the things they want, what happens next?"

"They soon want other things," Miss Hegarty said happily.

"And you give them what they want?"

"Oh yes, of course."

"Dear, dear, just fancy that," said the beastie, "and now I remember why I came here. It was because I wanted to."

"Not to stay!" Miss Hegarty gasped. The shop was full enough already.

"Why yes, to stay." The beastie smiled. "Now you mention it, I want to stay very much indeed. That is the only thing I do want. And everyone who comes here gets what they want, you told me that, didn't you?"

"Clever, aren't you?" said poor Miss Hegarty.

"Clever but clean about the house; I always wipe my feet," the beastie said.

What could Miss Hegarty do? "You can stay for a

week," she told him. So he stayed for a week. Miss Hegarty built him a little cave of his own in one corner of the shop, out of a couple of deckchairs, six bundles of firelighters, two bags of potatoes and the box of oranges. No one noticed him, for all the customers were too busy buying what they wanted from Miss Hegarty, and if the shop seemed a little more crowded than usual no one said anything about it.

At the end of the week Miss Hegarty opened the door of the shop very early in the morning before anyone was about and she moved away the two deckchairs. The beastie was sleeping very peacefully with his cheek in two of his six paws. He opened one eye.

"Now," said Miss Hegarty, "you came to visit me because you wanted to, and you have had what you wanted and it is time for you to go."

"Ah," said the beastie, "but wait a bit. There is something else that I want now. You said, didn't you, that there would be something else?"

"You want to go home, is that it?" Miss Hegarty suggested.

"Not to my home," said the beastie, "I want to come and live in your parlour at the back of the shop," and he looked at her softly and hopefully out of his green eyes. "Everyone who comes here gets what they want, didn't you say so?"

"Cunning, aren't you?" Miss Hegarty said.

"Cunning but comfortable, thank you very much," the beastie said.

What could Miss Hegarty do? "You can stay for a week in my parlour," she said. So for a week the beastie lived in the parlour at the back of the shop, in a special little corner between the piano and the pot of ferns, and he was very happy, especially when the radio played loud songs. He lay on his back waving time to the music with all six of his paws at once.

At the end of the week, very early in the morning before anyone in the village was about, Miss Hegarty came down to the parlour and moved away the pot of ferns.

"Now," she said, "you wanted to stay in my parlour and you have stayed in my parlour and it is time for you to go home."

"Ah," said the beastie, "but wait a bit. There is something else I want. You said, didn't you, that there would be something else? I want to stay for another week and sing to myself. I am tired of the noises that come out of that box."

"Conceited, aren't you?" said Miss Hegarty.

"Ah, but wait till you hear me singing," said the beastie.

What could Miss Hegarty do? For a week the beastie lay in her parlour, singing. Sometimes he sang sea-shanties, and sometimes he sang lullabies; sometimes

he sang as loud as a brass band and sometimes he sang as softly as the wind sings on a summer day. The people who came to the shop used to stop halfway down their shopping lists and ask Miss Hegarty what station her radio was tuned in to. Miss Hegarty pretended she didn't hear and hurried on to the next order, and slapped the bags of sugar down on the counter extra hard, to drown the sound of the beastie's voice.

At the end of the week, very very early in the morning, before even the birds were awake, Miss Hegarty went down to the parlour and said to the beastie, "You wanted to sing and you have sung and now you must stop singing. You must go home."

"Ah," said the beastie, and his green eyes shone like traffic lights, "there is one more thing that I want, just one. I am tired of singing when there is a piano here and no one playing it. I want you to play for me while I sing."

"To play for you? How can I play for you when all the people in the village are always coming into the shop wanting things?" she demanded.

"Think of it," the beastie said. "They all want things; all day long they want them, from morning to night – pepper and salt, sweets and string, ham, jam, needles and sewing thread; they want different things all the time. But I only want one thing."

"Well, I don't know – " Miss Hegarty said, and hesitated.

"I do," said the beastie, and smiled.

So Miss Hegarty sat down on the piano stool and she took some sheets of music from the top of the piano and set them on the music stand and she played – and she played – and she played.

The clock in the village struck nine. People with shopping baskets came to the door but the blind was still down. There were no rows of kettles and buckets sitting out on the pavement, no tin bath filled with bunches of flowers, no box of apples. How very strange! They rattled the door, knocked on the window, stamped their feet, jingled their money, bent down and looked through the slit in the blind and wondered what in the world could have happened.

That wasn't the sound of music they heard, was it? Could it be music? They went round to the garden gate at the side of the shop, and across the garden and then between the flower beds and up to the window of the parlour, and there they stood with their faces pressed close against the glass, gaping. This was where the music was coming from! At the piano, as happy as lords, Miss Hegarty and the beastie were singing duets.

If Pigs Could Fly

JAMES REEVES

If pigs could fly, I'd fly a pig
To foreign countries small and big –
To Italy and Spain,
To Austria, where cowbells ring,
To Germany, where people sing –
And then come home again.

I'd see the Ganges and the Nile,
I'd visit Madagascar's isle,
And Persia and Peru.
People would say they'd never seen
So odd, so strange an air-machine
As that on which I flew.

Why, everyone would raise a shout
To see his trotters and his snout
Come floating from the sky;
And I would be a famous star
Well known in countries near and far –
If only pigs could fly!